All inquiries should be addressed to:
Barron's Educational Series, Inc.
250 Wireless Boulevard
Hauppauge, NY 11788
http://www.barronseduc.com

Library of Congress Catalog Card No. 00-105773

ISBN-13: 978-0-7641-1764-0

Date of Manufacture : August 2018
Manufactured by : Shenzhen Wing King Tong Paper Products Co. Ltd.,
Shenzhen, Guangdong, China

Printed in China

39 38 37

I Miss You

A FIRST LOOK AT DEATH

PAT THOMAS
ILLUSTRATED BY LESLEY HARKER

BARRON'S

Every day someone is born...

and every day someone dies.

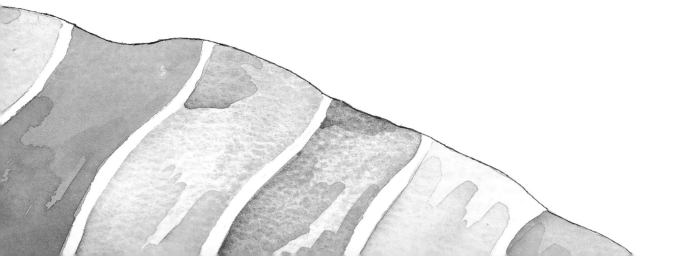

Death is a natural part of life. All living things grow, change, and eventually die.

8

When someone dies their body stops working – they stop breathing and their heart stops beating. They can't think or feel anymore. They don't eat or sleep.

In books and in movies, it is usually bad people who die. But in real life good people die, too.

People die for different reasons. Some people die because they are old. Some people get very sick and then they die. Some people die because something unexpected and tragic happened to them.

What about you?

Has anyone you know died? How did they die?

After a person dies there is usually a ceremony called a funeral.

At the funeral, people who knew that person can gather together to say good-bye. They may bring flowers, tell stories, or recite poems.

It can be hard to say good-bye
to someone you love.
It is normal to miss
them very much.

When someone dies, especially
if the death is sudden, it is
normal to think of things you
wish you had said, or things
you wish you had not said.

15

You may wish you had been nicer or
more helpful. But the way you
behaved did not make that person die.

Try to remind yourself that he or she died loving you for who you were, not for the things you did or said.

When someone you love dies it can feel
as if your heart has been torn in two.
It can feel as if part of you is missing.

These feelings can take a long time to get over.
You may feel lots of different sad feelings before
you finally begin to feel like yourself again.

What about you?

After someone dies it is normal to feel sad, angry,
guilty, afraid, and even happy. What are you feeling?

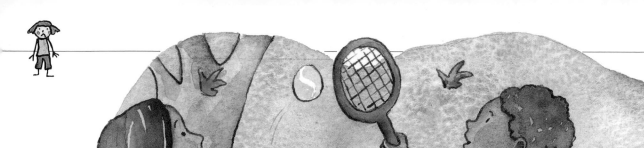

When someone you love dies, it can be hard to
do all the normal things you did before. You
may not feel like seeing your friends or joining
in groups. You may feel very alone.

Other people may find it hard to talk to you.
This is not because they don't care, but
because they don't know what to say
or do to help you.

What about you?

Do you have someone you can talk to when you are
feeling sad? What sort of things make you feel better right now?

There is a lot we don't know about death.
Every culture has different beliefs about
what happens after a person dies.

But most cultures also share some beliefs. Like the idea
that when a person dies their soul – the part of
them that made them special – takes a journey to join
the souls of other people who have passed away.

It's not an easy idea to understand.

Sometimes it helps if you think of the soul as a single raindrop, joining a great big ocean.

Even after someone you know or love dies, life goes on. The things you learned from that person stay inside of you and become a part of you.

As time goes on you will realize that
no one is completely gone as long as
you can remember the one you love.

HOW TO USE THIS BOOK

Children need to feel that they participated in the grieving that goes on after the death of someone close. If possible, try to encourage the child to make something for the person who has passed away that might be included in the burial ceremony. Or, if children are old enough, let them read a poem at the funeral.

When a family member dies, it can be very difficult for all members of the family to express their feelings. Life will not be normal for many months to come. Sometimes parents get so caught up in their own grief that they forget that their children are grieving, too. Try to remember that you are all in this together and that you all need each other's support. Death, especially if it is untimely, is difficult for adults to make sense of. It is even harder for children, who have much less experience in the world.

If the children are your own or close to you, then let them see you grieving. This is how they learn about handling grief. If they see you hiding grief away, that is what they will do. If they see you allowing grief to be a part of your life, then they too will be able to allow themselves to grieve. Let them mourn in your presence without having the need for it to make sense. Allow them to be sad without giving in to your natural inclination to make it better.

You may be the one that is grieving – for instance, if an old friend has just died. Using this book can help you explain to your children how you feel. But if they did not know the old friend very well, they may not experience the same depth of feeling. They may not feel anything at all.

Class projects about death are rare. Yet many children's lives are touched by death in one way or another. Individual children can be helped through the grieving process by being encouraged to make a special book about the person who has died. In it they can include drawings and photos. They can also record their thoughts about that person's death and their own feelings or memories. If your school is multicultural, you might get parents involved in talking about their different culture's beliefs about death. The idea is not to convince children that one belief or the other is right, but to allow a subject that is often taboo to be aired. This gives children the opportunity to think about death in a supportive way.

GLOSSARY

Funeral A memorial ceremony in which the person who has passed away is either buried or cremated. In a burial the body is usually placed in a box called a coffin and buried in the ground. In a cremation the body is burned and the ashes are returned to the family. The family may then place the ashes in a memorial, keep them at home, or scatter them somewhere special.

Soul The soul is the part of you that makes you special. You can't see the soul or touch it but everyone has one. Many cultures believe that even though the body dies the soul does not.

Grief Many people go through a period of grief after someone dies. Different people express grief in different ways. Some may feel very, very sad and tearful. Others feel tired, or lose their appetite and interest in doing things with their friends. Some feel very angry. Many people feel a mixture of these things.

FURTHER READING

Explaining Death to Children by Earl A. Grollman (Beacon Press, 1967)

Lost and Found by Rabbi Mark Gellman and Monsignor Thomas Hartman (Morrow Junior Books, 1999)

Part of Me Died, Too: Stories of Creative Survival Among Children and Teenagers by Virginia Lyn Fry (Dutton, 1995)

Talking About Death: A Dialogue Between Parent and Child by Earl A. Grollman (Beacon Press, 1976)

RESOURCES

The best way to find grief support for family members is by asking churches, hospitals, hospices, and mental health organizations in your community about locally available bereavement services. Also, elementary school counselors often run short-term bereavement groups for young children.